Who Is
Michael Jordan?

by Kirsten Anderson

illustrated by Dede Putra

Penguin Workshop

To my fellow Nets fans—who want everyone to know that we really do exist—KA

PENGUIN WORKSHOP
An Imprint of Penguin Random House LLC, New York

If you purchased this book without a cover, you should be aware that this book is stolen property. It was reported as "unsold and destroyed" to the publisher, and neither the author nor the publisher has received any payment for this "stripped book."

Visit us online at www.penguinrandomhouse.com.

Library of Congress Cataloging-in-Publication Data is available upon request.

ISBN 9780451532459 (paperback)   25 24 23 22 21 20 19
ISBN 9780451532473 (library binding)   10 9 8 7 6 5

Contents

Who Is Michael Jordan?

There was less than a minute to go in the 1982 college basketball championship game, one of the biggest events in sports. The Hoyas, Georgetown University's men's basketball team, had taken a one-point lead over their rivals, the Tar Heels from the University of North Carolina. With thirty-two seconds left, Carolina coach Dean Smith called a time-out so he could discuss their next moves with his players.

The team, in their white-and-blue uniforms, gathered around their coach. He knew that

Georgetown would carefully guard James Worthy and Sam Perkins, two UNC players who had become big stars. Coach Smith had to decide who else could take a shot at scoring a basket if Worthy and Perkins couldn't get free from defenders. He thought the team should try to get the ball to Michael.

Michael Jordan was a nineteen-year-old freshman at UNC in 1982. Coach Dean Smith rarely let freshmen play. He thought the first-year students needed to watch and learn—from the bench—before they were ready to play big-time college basketball.

But Michael stood out. He was quick and could jump high. He was tough and energetic. Even better, he loved to work and to learn. He practiced hard and listened to his coaches' instructions. Coach Smith knew he was different. He put Michael in the starting lineup for the first game of the season, and he stayed there all year.

Now, with seconds left on the clock, Coach Smith was going to trust the team's chance at a championship to the freshman, Michael Jordan. Everyone knew he had the talent to make the shot. But even more importantly, Michael had the confidence. Some athletes would be scared by this big moment. They might be afraid of making a mistake. And they certainly didn't want to be the one to lose the game. Michael was another kind of athlete. He *wanted* to take the shot.

The time-out ended and the players got ready to go back on the court. Their coach had only one thing to say: "Knock it in, Michael."

The clock started again. The Georgetown players swarmed Worthy and Perkins. Michael waited on the other side of the court. With fifteen seconds left, Jimmy Black passed the ball to him. Michael caught it and jumped in the air. The ball left his hands and sailed sixteen feet to the basket.

It swished in and the Tar Heels took a one-point lead. The crowd roared.

Georgetown had time to make another shot, but their players couldn't seem to score. The clock ticked down to zero. The UNC Tar Heels were the 1982 college basketball champions!

After the game, Michael told a reporter that he hadn't felt any pressure. It was just another jump shot.

That was the very first game-winning shot made by Michael Jordan. It was far from the last. He would go on to win six NBA championships and two Olympic gold medals. He was named Most Valuable Player five times and played on fourteen All-Star teams. Many people consider him the greatest basketball player ever and one of the greatest athletes of all time.

CHAPTER 1
Too Short

Michael Jeffrey Jordan was born in Brooklyn, New York, on February 17, 1963. His parents, James and Deloris, were both from North Carolina. James had moved the family to New York so that he could go to school. Michael had an older brother, James, known as Ronnie, and a sister, Deloris, called Sis. Another brother, Larry, was just a year older than him. The family returned to North Carolina when Michael was five months old. His sister Roslyn was born the next year.

In a family of five children, Michael wanted to be the center of attention. He danced, sang, told jokes, and played tricks. Sis said he always loved to have an audience.

The Jordans moved to Wilmington, North Carolina, when Michael was five so they could be closer to James's job at a General Electric plant. James loved baseball. He taught Michael and Larry to play as soon as they could hold a bat. Soon they were playing in Little League. As they got older, they also became interested in basketball. Their father put up a basketball hoop for the boys. And later he built a court for them.

When Michael was nine, he watched the 1972 Olympic gold medal basketball game between the United States and the Soviet Union. The Americans lost. Michael told his mother, "I'm going to be in the Olympics one day and I'm going to make sure we win."

James Naismith
and the Invention of Basketball

Dr. James Naismith (1861–1939) studied at McGill University and became a physical education teacher. In 1891, he took a job at the YMCA International Training School in Springfield, Massachusetts.

The head of the school asked Naismith to invent a game that would keep the restless young men active during the long, cold winter. Naismith nailed two peach baskets high on opposite walls and told players to try to score by tossing a soccer ball into the other team's basket. He also posted a list of thirteen rules. James Naismith had invented basketball!

The game quickly became popular. Naismith moved on to the University of Kansas to teach physical education. Many of the students he coached on the basketball team there became coaches themselves.

Naismith's influence is still felt today. The college player of the year is given the Naismith Award, and every year, new members are inducted into the Naismith Memorial Basketball Hall of Fame. Many of his original "thirteen rules" are still in use today.

Michael and Larry played against each other any chance they could get. Michael adored Larry and looked up to him, but he always wanted to beat him when they played.

Everyone agreed that Larry was a fantastic athlete. He was very strong and quick. Most people thought that Larry could have been a star basketball player. But there was one problem— everyone expected basketball players to be tall and Larry was short.

But Michael kept growing. Soon he was taller than Larry. He became an outstanding baseball player. At age twelve, he was named the state's most valuable player after his Little League team won the state championship.

He kept getting better at basketball, too. In 1977, Michael entered the ninth grade. Every morning, he came to the gym before school to practice basketball with his friend Leroy Smith. Michael was about five feet, seven inches tall. Leroy was a whole foot taller! But Michael was fast and could jump high. They had both made the middle school team. In one game, the team scored fifty-four points. Michael scored forty-four of them!

In 1978, Michael and Leroy began their sophomore year at Laney High School. They both tried out for the varsity basketball team. Leroy made it and Michael didn't. Later, the coaches said that they knew how good Michael was. But height is important in basketball. And the coaches felt that they needed someone tall like Leroy to compete with other teams.

But Michael didn't know the truth. He only knew that he hadn't made the team. He went home and cried alone in his room. He thought about quitting, but his mother encouraged him to stick with it. Michael took her advice and played with the junior varsity team during his first year at Laney. He worked hard and put on a show, averaging twenty-eight points per game. It was obvious how talented he was on the court.

Michael was worried, though. He wanted to have great skills *and* to be taller. He prayed every day. He hung from a bar, hoping to stretch himself out. By age sixteen, Michael was five feet ten. That was taller than most people in the Jordan family. It seemed unlikely he would grow much more than that.

Then one day, a cousin came to visit the Jordans. He was six feet seven! Suddenly Michael had hope—there were taller people than him in the family after all!

Michael had another worry as his sophomore year wore on. He had constant pain in his knees. His doctor took X-rays of Michael's legs and discovered good news. The X-rays showed that he was growing fast and had a lot more growing to do. The pain was probably related to his rapid growth.

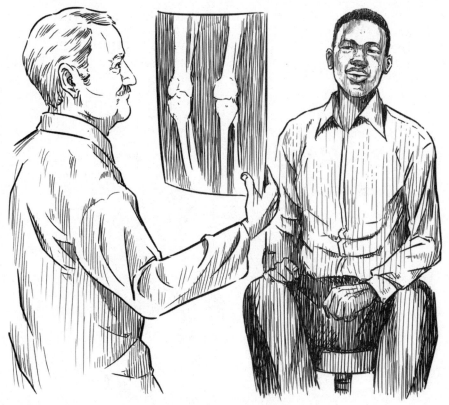

When he returned to school for his junior year in the fall of 1979, Michael was six feet three and still growing. He easily made the varsity team. Michael was offered two jersey numbers. He chose twenty-three because he hoped to be half as good a player as his brother Larry who wore number forty-five.

Now he had the height to match his skills. And people beyond his high school were beginning to notice.

CHAPTER 2
Carolina Blue

Word began to spread about the talented player at Laney High. The University of North Carolina had one of the best basketball teams in the country. They were interested in having Michael on their team. The coaches at UNC invited Michael to play at their summer camp for high-school basketball players.

North Carolina Tar Heels logo in 1979

Then they arranged for him to go to another basketball camp in Pittsburgh, Pennsylvania, that included some of the best basketball players in the country.

Michael was nervous at first. He was going

to play against other high-school kids from all over the United States. He thought of himself as just a small-town boy from North Carolina. How could he keep up with them?

He kept up with them just fine. The coaches and assistants at the Pittsburgh camp loved the way he ran hard to the basket and the extra kick he made as he jumped. They liked how he listened to the coaches. And they saw how much he wanted to win.

By the time the camp was over, Michael's name had jumped to the top of the lists of the best high-school players in the country.

For Michael, the summer camps were a turning point. Now he was certain he could go up against the best players. A few months earlier, he hadn't been sure if he would make a top college team. Now some people were saying he might be able to play in the NBA!

Michael didn't know what he would do if he couldn't be a basketball player. He even admitted that he was lazy about mostly everything except for sports! He got Bs and Cs in high school. He always tried to get out of doing his chores at home. He even quit his summer job at a hotel after only one week! His parents worried that he'd never be able to keep a job.

In November of his senior year of high school, Michael announced that he was going to accept a scholarship offer from UNC. The school would be paying Michael's tuition. He wanted to play for Coach Dean Smith. Two local TV stations came to the Jordans' house to broadcast the announcement.

The NBA

The National Basketball Association, or the NBA, is a men's professional basketball league that plays in North America. It began in 1946 as the Basketball Association of America, then merged in 1949 with the National Basketball League to form the NBA.

Today there are thirty teams in the NBA: twenty-nine in the United States and one in Canada. Teams play eighty-two games during a season that runs from October through mid-April. Then the playoffs start, and in June, two teams play for the NBA championship.

Michael arrived at UNC in the fall of 1981. At basketball practice, eighteen-year-old Michael talked constantly and loudly about how good he was and how he could beat the other players. He seemed like an annoying little brother. Michael's teammates just laughed it off most of the time. But sometimes they wondered how this loudmouth would fit in with college-level basketball and its rules.

Carolina basketball had many traditions. Coach Dean Smith was very strict. Clocks at practice kept players moving from one drill to another. The team worked hard to learn a system that

Dean Smith

highlighted defense and passing the ball.

But Michael loved it all. He liked the tightly

scheduled practices. He may have talked a lot, but he listened, too. Coach Smith's system didn't really show off Michael's athletic talents, but he didn't mind. He wanted to be known as a good defensive player. If the coach wanted him to pass the ball, he would. He always felt that his best skill was his willingness to listen and learn.

Some things bothered him, though. *Sports Illustrated* wanted to put UNC's starting five

players on its cover that fall before the season started. They wanted to include Michael. Dean Smith said no. He didn't think it was fair to put Michael on the cover when he hadn't even played in one game yet. Smith believed that each team member should wait their turn for a chance in the spotlight. It wasn't Michael's turn yet.

Michael was deeply angered by this. He thought he deserved to be a part of the cover photograph. But he never showed how he felt. Instead, he practiced harder. He listened and learned.

The 1981–82 season was about to open. Four returning players were set in the starting lineup. That left one spot open for Coach Smith to fill. The rest of the team would sit on the bench for most of each game, waiting and hoping for a chance to play.

Coach Smith posted the starting lineup right before the first game, and Michael's name was on it! He was set to start and play shooting guard.

Even he was shocked. Smith rarely started freshmen. But Michael seemed to be the best fit.

Michael wanted to show his coach that he had made the right choice. He scored the first points of that first game, and he continued to score as the season went on. He stuck with Smith's system and passed the ball to players who might be able to get an easier shot, even when he knew he could make the hard ones. He worked on his defense and made sure he was in the right place on the court.

In the spring of 1982, the Tar Heels found themselves in the running for a championship. UNC always did well in the tournament. But Dean Smith had never won a championship. And he had been the coach since 1961. Fans were growing impatient.

The 1982 championship was held at the Louisiana Superdome in New Orleans. The Georgetown Hoyas were a powerful team, and the score stayed close throughout the game. But after Michael made his big shot, UNC was the winner. And Michael was a star.

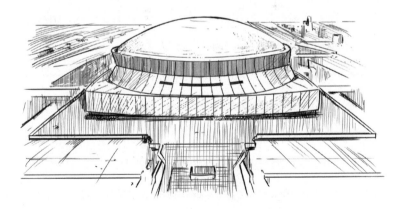

Louisiana Superdome in New Orleans

Positions on a Basketball Team

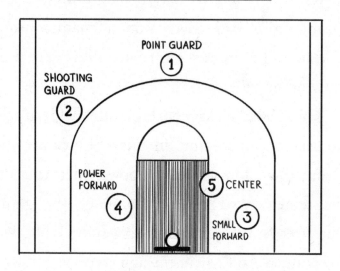

POINT GUARD

①

SHOOTING
GUARD

②

POWER
FORWARD

④

⑤ CENTER

SMALL ③
FORWARD

There are five players from each team on the court during a basketball game. Each player has a position with different responsibilities. The positions have names, but sometimes they are also called by their number.

- **Point Guard (1):** The point guard is responsible for running the *offense*—the system for scoring. The point guard leads the way in moving the ball down the court to the basket. Point guards are usually fast, and excel at passing the ball.

- Shooting Guard (2): The shooting guard focuses on scoring. They are often good at making shots from longer distances.
- Small Forward (3): The small forward is usually an excellent scorer who can shoot from different distances and who can also contribute to the defense.
- Power Forward (4): The power forward focuses on defense and rebounding—grabbing the ball after someone either makes or misses a shot. Power forwards are typically very strong and play close to the basket.
- Center (5): The center is the tallest player on the team. They score down near the basket as well as block the other team from scoring.

When Michael returned home to Wilmington for the summer, he was constantly surrounded by crowds. When he tried to play ball at the local courts, mobs would gather to watch. It seemed as if someone was always asking him for an autograph. Michael had become a hometown hero.

Although Michael hoped to win more championships at UNC, his sophomore and junior teams didn't even make it to the National Collegiate Athletic Association (NCAA) finals. He was deeply disappointed. Michael was named

Dr. James Naismith Award

the College Player of the Year in 1984. He also won the John R. Wooden Award and Dr. James Naismith Award, both for outstanding college player, in 1984. But he really just wanted to win another championship.

After his junior season,

Dean Smith advised Michael to move on to the NBA. Michael wasn't sure if it was the right thing to do. He still had another year of college to complete. He enjoyed being at UNC and still wanted to try to win another NCAA championship. Michael's mother was also against the idea. She wanted him to stay for his senior year and graduate from college.

But, finally, Michael decided that Coach Smith was right. He had had a great college career and the NBA had noticed. He was going to be drafted by a pro team. And he could always finish his degree later. It was time to go.

Michael and Coach Smith announce he is entering the NBA draft.

CHAPTER 3
Love of the Game

The NBA draft—where professional teams select college players—took place on June 19, 1984. The Houston Rockets picked first. Basketball teams at that time preferred to draft the tallest players they could find to play center.

That was considered the most important position on any team. The Rockets chose Hakeem Olajuwon (who was known as Akeem at the time), a seven-foot-tall player. The Portland Trail Blazers went next. They picked another big man, Sam Bowie. The

Chicago Bulls chose third. They also would
have liked to draft a tall center. But the two best
centers had already been chosen, and Michael's
talent was too great to ignore. The Bulls selected
Michael Jordan.

But before reporting to training camp with the Bulls in the fall, Michael had something even more important to do. The 1984 Summer Olympics were held in Los Angeles. And Michael had been one of twelve college players selected for the US basketball team! No professional players could join the Olympic team at that time.

Before the actual Olympics started, the teams played a series of games against NBA players. They traveled to nine different cities and faced groups of some of the best professional players in the league. The games were tough, but the Olympians won every game. Michael thought it was good preparation for the Olympics.

The United States beat Spain by thirty-one points in the gold medal game. After the game, Michael stood on the podium to receive his gold medal with the rest of the team. He sang the national anthem and held an American flag. After getting his gold medal, Michael ran into the stands and gave it to his mother.

He reminded her of how he had promised to win a gold medal for the United States when he was nine years old. Now he had done it.

After the Olympics, Michael signed his first contract to play for the Chicago Bulls. They agreed to pay him $6 million over seven years.

It was the third biggest contract in NBA history. His contract with the Bulls had a special "love of the game" clause. Most NBA contracts said that players couldn't play in non-NBA games or do anything that might cause an injury. Teams wanted to be sure that their players stayed healthy. But Michael was allowed to play anytime he wanted. He could join a pickup game in a park or a gym without the risk of losing his contract. He was the only player who had this clause in his contract. Michael was twenty-one years old, and he just wanted to play basketball, anytime and anywhere.

Michael's agent told him that some people at the Nike company wanted to talk to him about basketball sneakers. Nike had been known mostly for its running shoes but was trying to establish itself with new basketball gear. The company promised to design a special shoe and athletic clothing for Michael. It wanted him to appear in its ads and commercials. Nike was ready to build a whole group of products around Michael Jordan. The company had even chosen a name for the brand: "Air Jordan."

In 1984, Michael preferred to wear Adidas shoes. He didn't even want to meet with the Nike representatives! But his parents made him go to the meeting. They thought the Nike deal was a

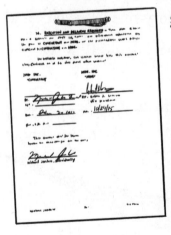

good one. Finally, Michael agreed to listen to Nike and accepted the offer. He would be paid $2.5 million over five years, and would receive even more money for each pair of Air Jordans sold.

People in the basketball world were shocked. That was an awful lot of money and attention for a young man who hadn't even played one game in the NBA yet!

Nike knew it was taking a risk. But the company thought Michael had the talent and personality to become a star.

CHAPTER 4
The Rookie

During the 1970s, many people had lost interest in professional basketball. They didn't follow the game or the players. Some NBA playoff games weren't even shown live on TV! NBA management was working hard on bringing fans back to the game when Michael joined the organization in 1984.

Earvin "Magic" Johnson of the Los Angeles Lakers and Larry Bird of the Boston Celtics began to draw crowds with their flashy skills and on-court rivalry. They helped make the NBA fun again. Fans loved the two stars and their games against each other. Many believe that the Magic-Bird rivalry helped save the NBA after it had lost popularity in the 1970s.

Magic Johnson and Larry Bird

When the Celtics beat the Lakers for the NBA championship in 1984, the Chicago Bulls were one of the worst teams in the league. Even the local TV stations and newspapers rarely paid attention to them. Chicago Stadium was old and usually half-empty during Bulls games.

The Sneaker Commercial That Changed a Basketball Rivalry

In 1985, the Converse shoe company asked Magic Johnson to make a television commercial with Larry Bird. Magic was nervous. Although he and Bird had been fierce rivals for years, they had never actually had a conversation!

During a break in filming, Bird invited Magic to have lunch at his house. The two men soon realized they had a lot in common. They were both from the Midwest. They both grew up in poor families. They cared about basketball more than almost anything. They actually liked each other!

The Converse commercial—featuring both the Bird Shoe and the Magic Shoe—was a success. And the two former rivals remained friends.

Larry Bird

Magic Johnson

Michael didn't care about any of that, though. He was ready to play basketball. He played as if every game was a championship game. He practiced the same way. People around the league noticed. Fans, reporters, and even other players were all talking about the high-flying rookie.

That season, Michael played in his first Nike shoes. They were mostly red and black to match the Bulls' uniforms. The NBA rules said that players must have a certain amount of white on their shoes. They fined Michael for breaking the NBA rules every time he wore his "Jordans."

Nike offered to pay Michael's fines, and it turned out to be great publicity for the shoes *and* the team. People were already interested in Michael's sneakers. The fact that they were "illegal" by NBA rules made them even more cool. When the Air Jordan 1 shoes were first sold to the public in 1985, they were an instant hit, earning $105 million in less than a year.

Now it's common for basketball stars to sign deals for their own brand of sneakers. But Air Jordans were the ones that started it all.

Fans were excited about Michael, but some other NBA players didn't like the new young player much. They were jealous of the deal he had with Nike. At the 1985 All-Star Game—when most basketball players just wore their uniforms and plain team warm-ups—Michael wore his flashy new Air Jordan warm-up suit and gold chains to the slam-dunk contest!

The other players thought Michael looked like someone who was more interested in being a star and promoting his brand than in playing basketball.

The Bulls made the playoffs in 1985, but lost in the first round. Although Michael won Rookie of the Year, it didn't seem to matter that much to him. He really just wanted his team to win.

Air Jordans

In 1985, a pair of Air Jordan 1s cost around sixty-five dollars, which was a lot of money for sneakers at the time. Many kids dreamed of being able to buy their first pair of Jordans.

Hip-hop stars rapped about Air Jordans and wore them onstage and in music videos. Movie stars wore them with tuxedos. Michael was young and cool. People wanted to wear his shoes and feel cool, too.

LL Cool J

New Air Jordan models were released each year. People began to collect them. Nike sold only a limited number of each model the first day, which forced people to wait in line for hours outside of stores, hoping to get the latest pair. Air Jordans helped create a culture of *sneakerheads*—people who are obsessed with collecting sneakers.

CHAPTER 5
Trust No One

During the third game of the 1985–86 season, Michael landed hard coming down from a jump. X-rays showed that he had broken his foot. It could take weeks, or even months, to heal. He had never before missed a game for any reason.

Michael went back to college while his foot was healing. He took classes at UNC to finish his degree. After a few months, he returned to the Bulls. But he could play only a few minutes during each game because of the injury. With Michael back, the Bulls won just enough games to make the playoffs again. And this time they had to play Larry Bird and the powerful Boston Celtics in the first round.

During the second game, Michael scored sixty-three points! That was a record for most points in a single playoff game. But the Celtics won that game and the series. Michael alone wasn't enough to win a championship for the Bulls.

Michael pushed harder than ever the next year. He scored twenty, thirty, or even forty points a night. Audiences cheered his tough defense, quick moves, and high-flying dunks. Michael could jump as high as four feet with no problem. He truly was "Air Jordan"! Chicago Stadium was now packed for every game. Ticket sales soared at other arenas when the Bulls came to town.

The Chicago Bulls warm up before a game.

Many people had never seen a player as exciting as Michael.

And Michael was just as popular off the court. He continued to earn millions from the sales of Air Jordans. His contracts with other companies, such as McDonald's, Coca-Cola, and Chevrolet, paid him much more money than his NBA contract.

Michael had become so famous that he couldn't go anywhere without being mobbed by fans. Even people who weren't basketball fans recognized him from his television commercials. The golf course became one of the few places he

Juanita Vanoy

could go where crowds didn't follow him. He had a close circle of family and friends from UNC and Wilmington. And he was engaged to his girlfriend, Juanita Vanoy, whom he had met a year earlier. But it was clear he couldn't lead an ordinary life anymore.

Michael won the Most Valuable Player award and Defensive Player of the Year for the 1987–88 season. In 1988, Nike introduced a new Air Jordan logo that everyone called "Jumpman." It was a silhouette of Michael jumping in the air.

To promote the new
Jumpman sneakers,
Michael made a series of
TV commercials for Nike
with the young film director
Spike Lee. They were short,
funny, black-and-white ads that really boosted
the popularity of Air Jordans.

On November 18, 1988, Juanita gave birth
to her and Michael's first child, Jeffrey Michael
Jordan. The new family moved into a large house
in Highland Park, a suburb of Chicago.

The Bulls kept adding new players and changing coaches. They made the playoffs, but didn't win. Michael was getting frustrated. He felt like he needed to do all the scoring. He didn't believe he could trust the other players' skills. Some people thought that Michael Jordan might never win a championship if he kept trying to do it all himself.

CHAPTER 6
Three-peat

After the 1988–89 season ended, Michael and Juanita went on a trip to California. They made a side trip to Las Vegas, where they got married.

The Bulls had a new coach when Michael returned to training camp for the beginning of the 1989–90 season. Phil Jackson had been an assistant coach for the Bulls. He had played in the NBA in the 1970s. He was known for being a deep thinker who liked to try different things. Jackson thought of himself as a defensive coach. His assistant, Tex Winter, took over coaching the offense.

Phil Jackson

Coach Winter taught the Bulls his "triangle offense" system. It involved sharing the ball and moving around the court in a specific way.

Michael was unsure. He thought he was the only one who could make the big shots. Jackson told him he would need to learn to trust his teammates.

But that was difficult for Michael.

The Bulls made it to the Eastern Conference Finals once again, only to lose the series. After the game, Michael cried. He had no idea what it would take to win the championship.

Eventually, Coach Winter's system began to work. Michael found ways to use it to his advantage. The other players understood it now, too. The team's stronger defense also helped. And Scottie Pippen, a talented player who came to the Bulls in 1987, was now a star himself. He made the Bulls a better team.

In 1991, the Chicago Bulls went back to the Eastern Conference Finals to play the Detroit Pistons for the third year in a row. This time, the Bulls swept them in four games.

Scottie Pippen

They faced the Los Angeles Lakers and their star Magic Johnson. The Bulls shocked everyone by winning the series in just five games. They were finally the NBA champions!

Magic Johnson

It had taken seven years for Michael and his team to win the championship. He cried as he held the trophy.

In August 1991, Michael starred in a Gatorade commercial. It featured a song with the words "Like Mike . . . If I could be like Mike." Every kid wanted to be like Mike. Michael Jordan had become a huge star, both on and off the court.

The Bulls went to the NBA Finals again in 1992. They played the Portland Trail Blazers. In game one, Michael scored thirty-five points in the first half and made six three-point shots. Both were records. The Bulls won the series in six games.

Soon after the NBA Finals in June, Michael began to prepare for the Summer Olympics in Barcelona, Spain. The Olympic rules had changed and for the first time, the US team included mostly NBA players.

The all-star US basketball team was nicknamed the "Dream Team." Crowds went crazy wherever they went. Players on other countries' teams asked for autographs and pictures before each game.

Charles Barkley and Magic Johnson sign autographs for players on Team Croatia.

The "Dream Team"

The 1992 US Olympic basketball team featured some of the most impressive players in the sport. They were:

- Charles Barkley (Phoenix Suns)
- Larry Bird (Boston Celtics)
- Clyde Drexler (Portland Trail Blazers)
- Patrick Ewing (New York Knicks)

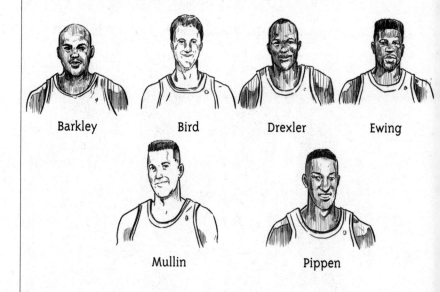

Barkley   Bird   Drexler   Ewing

Mullin   Pippen

- **Magic Johnson (Los Angeles Lakers)**
- **Michael Jordan (Chicago Bulls)**
- **Christian Laettner (Duke University)**
- **Karl Malone (Utah Jazz)**
- **Chris Mullin (Golden State Warriors)**
- **Scottie Pippen (Chicago Bulls)**
- **David Robinson (San Antonio Spurs)**
- **John Stockton (Utah Jazz)**
- **Coach: Chuck Daly (Detroit Pistons)**

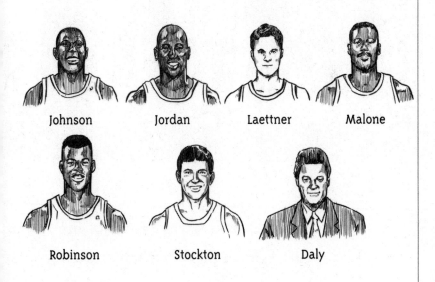

Johnson   Jordan   Laettner   Malone

Robinson   Stockton   Daly

The United States easily won most of its
games. The toughest games they played were often

against each other at practice. The Dream Team
won the gold medal, as everyone had expected.

The 1992–93 season was tough, but the Bulls made the Finals again. They faced the Phoenix Suns and won their third championship in six difficult games. People called the three championships a "three-peat."

Michael was exhausted. Although he was just thirty years old, he had made comments throughout the season about retiring soon. No one believed him, though.

CHAPTER 7
Now Batting . . . Michael Jordan

By 1993, Michael had won three championships and many individual awards. He and Juanita had two more children: Marcus, born in 1990, and Jasmine, born in 1992. He was one of the most popular athletes in the world. Then tragedy struck during the summer of 1993. His father was killed during a robbery.

Michael was heartbroken over his father's death. They had always been close. As Michael had become more and more famous, his father was one of the few people he could really talk to. And now he was gone.

Michael wasn't up to another eighty-two-game season with the Bulls. On October 6, 1993, Michael announced his retirement from professional basketball.

Everyone was shocked. It was hard to believe that the sport's biggest star would suddenly quit. What would Michael do next?

Basketball might have run out of challenges for him. But other sports, like baseball, still held plenty.

Jerry Reinsdorf, who owned the Chicago White Sox baseball team, offered Michael an invitation to spring training camp to find out what he could do.

Jerry Reinsdorf

Michael practiced hitting on his own for a few months, then traveled to training camp in Florida. He hadn't played baseball since high school. The muscles he used for basketball were different than those he needed for baseball. His height was an advantage in basketball, but it made baseball more difficult. He had to start over.

But Michael always liked to work hard. He arrived early to the ball field each day and stayed later than everyone else. When his coaches told him something, he listened and did whatever they asked.

It wasn't easy, though. Michael struggled, even with all his hard work. It was the first time in a long time that he wasn't the best at what he was doing.

Michael spent the 1994 season with the Birmingham Barons, a minor-league team in Alabama. He wore number forty-five, his brother Larry's old high-school number. He took long bus trips and carried his own equipment, just like other minor-league players. He said baseball made him feel like a kid again. He felt his father was with him, just as he had been at Little League.

But he wasn't *really* just like other minor leaguers. Cameras and reporters followed Michael's every move. People traveled from far away to see Michael play baseball. No other minor-league player got as much attention as Michael.

Michael began to improve. His manager believed Michael might have a chance to make the major-league White Sox team in a few years. Michael thought he could make it even sooner.

A Major League Baseball players' strike at the end of 1994 dragged on into spring training in 1995. Michael became impatient. He didn't want to be involved in the strike and the conflict between players and team owners. He quit baseball on March 10.

He felt it had been a good experience, though. Baseball had reminded Michael of what it was like to have to work hard at a sport. But he was ready to go back to the game he excelled at.

Michael began to practice again with the Bulls. On March 18, 1995, he sent out a press release. It simply said, "I'm back."

CHAPTER 8
Three-peat, Part 2

The Chicago Bulls now played in a new, modern stadium. They had a statue of Michael outside of it! When he retired, his jersey number,

twenty-three, had also been retired. That meant no one else could wear that number. So Michael returned to the court wearing forty-five, his baseball number. He was a little rusty in his first few games. But then the team traveled to New York City to play the New York Knicks at Madison Square Garden.

Michael always loved playing basketball at the Garden. The spotlight was bright there. The crowds were loud, and lots of celebrities came to watch.

Michael scored fifty-five points that night. Everyone thought that he was really back in the game.

But Michael missed some shots he used to make easily. The Bulls had changed a lot while he was playing baseball. There were many new players who found it hard to play—or even practice—with Michael.

The Bulls won the first round of the playoffs but struggled in the second round against the Orlando Magic. After one game, a Magic player said, "Number forty-five is not number twenty-

Orlando Magic player Nick Anderson

three." Michael went back to wearing number twenty-three for the next game, and the Bulls won.

The Bulls lost the series, though. Michael was disappointed. He hadn't played well and had made mistakes. He knew he needed to work hard to get ready for the next year.

But he had to get ready for Hollywood, too. Michael was cast to star in a movie called *Space Jam* with the cartoon character Bugs Bunny. The two had already starred in Nike ads playing basketball together. Bugs Bunny wore

"Hare Jordans" in the commercials. *Space Jam* was released in 1996. It was a huge hit, earning $230.4 million worldwide to date.

While working on *Space Jam*, Michael had a basketball court built

next to the movie studio. He practiced every time he had a break during the film shoot. Soon, other NBA players began to stop by the court when they were in Los Angeles. Michael got a chance to play against all-stars almost every day.

After filming ended, Michael was excited for the beginning of the next basketball season. The Bulls had made one key change: They added Dennis Rodman, one of the best rebounders in the league. He was famous for his crazy stunts off the court but his Bulls teammates found Dennis to be quiet and hardworking.

Dennis Rodman

Michael seemed more driven than ever. He wanted to prove that he could still win. He pushed his teammates hard during practice. Some of them found it difficult to work with him.

The team managed to come together at game time, though. They won a record seventy-two games during the 1995–96 season.

The Bulls defeated the Seattle SuperSonics in six games to win the NBA Finals. The last game took place on Father's Day. After they won, Michael grabbed the game ball and cried in the locker room. The memory of his father and the pressure he had put on himself to win overwhelmed him.

But Michael immediately promised that the

Bulls would be back next year to win another championship. And they were.

The Bulls faced the Utah Jazz in the 1997 NBA Finals. After four games, the series was tied 2–2.

Michael woke up sick the morning of game five. He had the flu. He didn't go to practice. Instead, he spent the day with the team trainer, trying to find ways to feel better. People wondered if he would even be able to play.

Michael was sick, dizzy, and dehydrated. But he played anyway, scoring thirty-eight points. The Bulls won.

They had a chance to win the series in game six. Michael had the ball near the end of the game. Jazz players swarmed around him. But instead of trying a difficult shot, he passed the ball to a teammate, Steve Kerr, who made the winning basket. Michael finally trusted his teammates. He didn't always have to take the big shot.

Steve Kerr

The 1997–98 season wasn't easy. The team fought its way to the playoffs. They faced the Jazz again in the Finals and got to game six again. The clock ticked down toward zero. Scottie Pippen passed the ball to Michael. He took a shot and it swished through the basket.

Michael seemed to freeze in midair, holding the pose for a few seconds, as if someone had made a statue of him taking the perfect shot. The game ended and the Bulls were champions once again. With Michael, they had completed two sets of championship "three-peats," from 1991–1993 and from 1996–1998. It would be a hard act to follow.

CHAPTER 9
Wizard

After the 1998 championship, Scottie Pippen was traded away from the Bulls. And Phil Jackson left the team.

The NBA owners and the players' association were in a conflict about contracts and money. So the season didn't start until they came to an agreement in January 1999.

On January 13, Michael announced—yet again—that he was retiring from the Bulls. He was exhausted. And he felt that the time was right to leave the team.

In 2000, the Washington Wizards offered Michael a chance to become president of basketball operations and a part owner of the team. He would be responsible for drafting, signing, and trading the players on the team. He also would hire coaches.

But after a few months, Michael decided that the only way to get the players to work hard would be to show them himself. He was out of shape, and his knees hurt from all the years of running and jumping. But he believed he could get himself ready for the next season. He had to give up his partial ownership of the team so that he could play with the Wizards.

Michael announced his return to basketball at the end of September 2001.

During practice, he went back to bossing the younger players. But some of them just didn't care, which upset Michael. As always, he only wanted to win. His knees hurt every day, but he still pushed himself. He scored fifty-one points in one game—just before his thirty-ninth birthday.

He made the All-Star team in 2002 and 2003. But everyone could see that Michael was in a lot of pain. He thought he would retire and go back to being the president and part owner of the Wizards.

He was wrong. The Wizards owner didn't think he'd done a good job building the team. For the first time ever, someone fired Michael Jordan.

CHAPTER 10
The Greatest

In 2006, Michael officially joined the Charlotte Bobcats. Team owner Robert L. Johnson offered Michael partial ownership and  put him in charge of basketball operations. The Bobcats were a new team in Charlotte, North Carolina. They replaced the Hornets, who had moved to New Orleans in 2002.

Michael's personal life also changed in 2006. He and Juanita divorced. They had separated once before, in 2002, but had gotten back together. This time it was final.

It was tough to make the Bobcats into a winning team. Fans didn't always agree with

Michael's draft choices and trades. The team lost a lot of games.

It was hard being in charge of a team. But everyone still remembered Michael's playing career. He was inducted into the Basketball Hall of Fame in 2009. At the Hall of Fame ceremony, he was expected to make a speech. He was nervous about the event. The audience was filled with people who had been helpful and important to his career. When others spoke about him, he became emotional and cried several times. Then, it was time for Michael to give his own speech.

It was a disaster. Michael wanted to explain why he was so competitive. And so he began by talking about the times people had doubted him or slighted him. He told the story of when Leroy Smith made the varsity basketball team and he didn't. He spoke about the time Dean Smith wouldn't let him be on the *Sports Illustrated* cover.

People were horrified. Hall of Fame speeches were usually warm and filled with gratitude. Michael's just seemed bitter and angry. But he wanted to let people know that those slights and doubts were the things that pushed him to be greater at the sport.

He did thank many people in the speech. But most of all, he thanked the game itself. He said: "The game of basketball has been everything to me. My refuge. My place I've always gone when I needed to find comfort and peace."

In 2010, Michael bought Robert Johnson's share of the Bobcats. He became the first former player to solely own an NBA team. The team's finances improved. He donated money to keep sports programs going for local middle schools and helped get the team's players involved in the community.

But the Bobcats seemed to get even worse on the court. Michael hired another executive to take over basketball operations, but they kept losing.

Coaches came and went. Fans and sportswriters criticized his decisions. Some called him the worst owner in the league! Others said he should sell the team.

Then, in 2013, he made one move that everyone did like. The New Orleans Hornets changed their name to the Pelicans. Jordan asked the NBA if Charlotte could have the Hornets name back. The league granted his request and they became the Charlotte Hornets again.

Michael's personal life was also changing. After dating for a few years, he married Yvette Prieto in 2013. The next year, Michael and Yvette had twin daughters, Victoria and Ysabel.

From 2015 to 2016, more than 50 percent of all basketball sneakers sold in the United States were from the Jordan Brand of Nikes. Michael earned $100 million a year from his Nike deal alone. In 2015, he was named to *Forbes* magazine's list of billionaires. He is the highest-paid athlete of all time, with $1.85 billion in total earnings—$93 million of it from his playing career. He is still one of the most popular athletes in the world. In 2016, he received the Presidential Medal of Freedom from President Barack Obama.

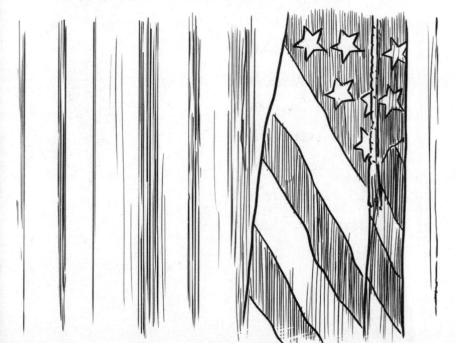

When an *ESPN The Magazine* reporter did a long interview with Michael before his fiftieth birthday, Michael spoke about how his whole life had been about competition and how hard it was not to play anymore. He asked, "How can I find peace away from the game of basketball?" He hadn't found an answer yet.

Michael Jordan has been called the greatest basketball player of all time and one of history's greatest athletes. He always worked hard to make the most of his natural talent.

He always demanded the best of himself and the best of those around him.

Michael Jordan changed the NBA with his high-flying airborne style and speed. He changed the world of advertising, too. Before Michael, few basketball players were ever seen in advertisements. Now they are everywhere.

LeBron James

Michael's career is filled with highlights that astonished fans at the time and still continue to do so. Sometimes Michael startled himself by what he could do. Once he told a reporter how watching one of his dunks on video in slow motion made him feel. He wondered, aloud, "When does jumping become flying?"

When it's Michael Jordan.

Awards and Accomplishments

- Five-time NBA Most Valuable Player (1988, 1991, 1992, 1996, 1998)
- Six-time NBA Finals Most Valuable Player (1991–93, 1996–98)
- Ten-time All-NBA First Team (1987–93, 1996–98)
- All-NBA Second Team (1985)
- Nine-time NBA All-Defensive First Team (1988–93, 1996–98)
- NBA Defensive Player of the Year (1988)
- NBA Rookie of the Year (1985)
- NBA All-Rookie First Team (1985)
- Three-time NBA All-Star Game MVP (1988, 1996, 1998)
- Fourteen NBA All-Star Game selections
- Recorded only triple-double in All-Star Game history (fourteen points, eleven rebounds, and eleven assists) at the 1997 NBA All-Star Game in Cleveland

- Won All-Star Weekend Slam Dunk Contest in 1987 and 1988
- Holds the NBA record for highest points per game average (minimum 400 games or 10,000 points)—31.5
- Holds the NBA Finals record for highest single-series scoring average—41.0 points per game (1993)
- Holds the NBA Finals single-game record for most points in one half—35 (June 3, 1992, versus Portland)
- NBA record for most points in a playoff game (sixty-three points against the Boston Celtics on April 20, 1986)
- Olympic gold medalist in men's basketball (1984, 1992)

Timeline of Michael Jordan's Life

1963 — Born February 17 in Brooklyn, New York

1982 — Scores winning points for the University of North Carolina Tar Heels in NCAA championship game

1984 — Leaves UNC to enter the NBA draft; selected third by the Chicago Bulls

— Wins both the Naismith Award and the Wooden Award for college player of the year

1985 — Wins Rookie of the Year

1988 — Wins MVP and Defensive Player of the Year

1989 — Marries Juanita Vanoy

1991 — Wins first NBA championship with the Chicago Bulls

1992 — Wins gold medal as a member of US Olympic "Dream Team"

1994 — Plays baseball for Minor League Baseball team the Birmingham Barons

1995 — Returns to NBA and the Chicago Bulls

1996 — Stars in the movie *Space Jam*

2000 — Becomes president of basketball operations and part owner of the Washington Wizards

2006 — Becomes president of basketball operations and part owner of the Charlotte Bobcats

— Divorces Juanita

2013 — Marries Yvette Prieto

2016 — Receives the Presidential Medal of Freedom from President Barack Obama

Timeline of the World

1963 — Martin Luther King Jr. gives his "I Have a Dream" speech

1964 — The Civil Rights Act is passed

1969 — Neil Armstrong becomes the first person to walk on the moon

1974 — President Richard M. Nixon resigns

1980 — The *Pac-Man* video game is released

1982 — Michael Jackson releases *Thriller*

1984 — LeBron James is born in Akron, Ohio

1985 — The wreck of the *Titanic* is found off the coast of Newfoundland

1990 — The biggest art theft in history takes place at the Gardner Museum in Boston

1994 — The "Chunnel," connecting Britain and France, opens

1997 — The first Harry Potter book is published

2001 — The September 11 attacks kill almost three thousand people in the United States

2007 — The iPhone debuts

2008 — Barack Obama is elected the first African American president of the United States

2016 — The Chicago Cubs win the World Series for the first time in 108 years

Bibliography

Badenhausen, Kurt. "How Michael Jordan Still Makes $100 Million a
    Year," *Forbes*, March 11, 2015. https://www.forbes.com/sites/
    kurtbadenhausen/2015/03/11/how-new-billionaire-michael-
    jordan-earned-100-million-in-2014/#395f7c2b221a.

Badenhausen, Kurt. "Michael Jordan Heads the Highest-
    Paid Athletes of All-Time with $1.7 Billion," *Forbes*,
    December 6, 2016. https://www.forbes.com/sites/
    kurtbadenhausen/2016/12/06/michael-jordan-heads-
    the-highest-paid-athletes-of-all-time-with-1-7-
    billion/#11c0f36e1f1d.

Halberstam, David. *Playing for Keeps: Michael Jordan and the
    World He Made.* New York: Random House, 1999.

Jordan, Michael. *For the Love of the Game: My Story.* Edited by
    Mark Vancil. New York: Crown Publishers, 1998.

Lazenby, Roland. *Michael Jordan: The Life.* New York: Back Bay
    Books, 2015.

McCallum, Jack. ***Dream Team: How Michael, Magic, Larry, Charles, and the Greatest Team of All Time Conquered the World and Changed the Game of Basketball Forever.*** New York: Ballantine Books, 2012.

McCallum, Jack. "'The Desire Isn't There,'" ***Sports Illustrated***, October 18, 1993. http://www.si.com/vault/1993/10/18/129606/michael-jordan-the-desire-isnt-there.

Smith, Sam. ***The Jordan Rules.*** New York: Simon & Schuster, 1992.

Thompson, Wright. "Michael Jordan Has Not Left the Building," ***ESPN The Magazine***, February 22, 2013. http://www.espn.com/espn/feature/story/_/page/Michael-Jordan/michael-jordan-not-left-building.

Zwerling, Jared. "'I'm Back!': Untold Tales of Michael Jordan's 1st Return to the NBA 20 Years Ago," ***Bleacher Report***, March 18, 2015. http://bleacherreport.com/articles/2389936-im-back-untold-tales-of-michael-jordans-1st-return-to-the-nba-20-years-ago.